SPECIAL REPORTS

HATE CRIMES IN AMERICA

BY MELISSA ABRAMOVITZ

CONTENT CONSULTANT
JEANNINE BELL
RICHARD S. MELVIN PROFESSOR OF LAW
MAURER SCHOOL OF LAW
INDIANA UNIVERSITY–BLOOMINGTON

Essential Library
An Imprint of Abdo Publishing | abdopublishing.com

abdopublishing.com

Published by Abdo Publishing, a division of ABDO, PO Box 398166, Minneapolis, Minnesota 55439. Copyright © 2017 by Abdo Consulting Group, Inc. International copyrights reserved in all countries. No part of this book may be reproduced in any form without written permission from the publisher. Essential Library™ is a trademark and logo of Abdo Publishing.

Printed in the United States of America, North Mankato, Minnesota
102016
012017

Cover Photo: Joe Scarnici/WireImage/Getty Images
Interior Photos: Chuck Burton/AP Images, 4–5; Grace Beahm/The Post and Courier/AP Images, 8; A. Katz/Shutterstock Images, 13; Ivan Bliznetsov/iStockphoto, 14–15; Clem Albers/US National Archives and Records Administration, 18; Sanford Myers/The Tennessean/AP Images, 22; Erik K. Lesser/EPA European Pressphoto Agency b.v./Alamy, 26–27; Jacquelyn Martin/AP Images, 30, 70; Rene Macura/AP Images, 36; North Wind Picture Archives, 38–39; AP Images, 42; Paul Sancya/AP Images, 48; Hulton Archive/Getty Images, 50–51; OFF/AFP/Getty Images, 55; Steve Liss/The LIFE Images Collection/Getty Images, 59; Chip Somodevilla/Getty Images, 62–63, 88–89; Robert Sherbow/The LIFE Images Collection/Getty Images, 66; Mike Derer/AP Images, 72–73; Chris Maddaloni/CQ Roll Call/AP Images, 77; Al Maglio/The Kirksville Daily Express/AP Images, 80–81; Mel Evans/AP Images, 85; Mark Welsh/Daily Herald/AP Images, 93; David Goldman/AP Images, 96; Loren Elliott/The Tampa Bay Times/AP Images, 99

Editor: Arnold Ringstad
Series Designer: Maggie Villaume

Publisher's Cataloging-in-Publication Data

Names: Abramovitz, Melissa, author.
Title: Hate crimes in America / by Melissa Abramovitz.
Description: Minneapolis, MN : Abdo Publishing, 2017. | Series: Special reports |
    Includes bibliographical references and index.
Identifiers: LCCN 2016945216 | ISBN 9781680783964 (lib. bdg.) |
    ISBN 9781680797497 (ebook)
Subjects: LCSH: Hate crimes--United States--Juvenile literature.
Classification: DDC 364.150973--dc23
LC record available at http://lccn.loc.gov/2016945216

CONTENTS

CHAPTER ONE

THE CHARLESTON
MASSACRE

At approximately 8:00 p.m. on June 17, 2015, 21-year-old Dylann Roof entered the historic Emanuel African Methodist Episcopal (AME) Church in Charleston, South Carolina. Roof, who is white, was warmly welcomed by 12 African-American participants in a Bible study group. Approximately one hour later, Roof pulled out a .45-caliber handgun and began shooting, killing nine people and injuring another.[1] Survivors say before he started the rampage, he stated, "You are raping our women and taking over our country."[2] He also used racial slurs.

Roof's victims ranged in age from 26 to 87. They included several pastors, a state senator, and a speech therapist. They all shared a deep faith and commitment

The Emanuel AME Church, one of the nation's oldest black churches, was established in 1816.

to their church. They were mothers, fathers, grandparents, sons, and daughters. The shootings devastated their families and community. But Roof saw them only as an inferior class of people who he believed were taking over America. In a manifesto he published online, he explained that he hoped to start a race war. He chose to do this at one of the oldest African-American churches in the United States. Emanuel AME Church has played a big role in African Americans' civil rights struggles and triumphs. The Reverend Martin Luther King Jr. is one of many prominent people who has spoken at the church.

THE AFTERMATH

Roof fled after the shootings and drove to North Carolina,

WHO IS DYLANN ROOF?

Dylann Roof grew up spending time in both parents' middle-class homes. He attended racially integrated schools. Roof's friend Caleb Brown, who is biracial, told the *New York Times* Mrs. Roof welcomed him into their home. During Roof's high school years, his parents had personal and financial problems that led him to struggle in school. He dropped out of high school. Taliaferro Robinson-Heyward, a middle-school friend, remembered, "When he opened up, you could tell something was wrong at home . . . . It wasn't like he was a mean person, but you could tell he had a darkness to his life."[3]

After that, Roof held odd jobs and began abusing alcohol and drugs. He also had minor run-ins with the police. After the 2012 Trayvon Martin shooting, Roof connected with white supremacist groups. His friends said he talked about starting a race war, but until the Charleston murders, he had no record of violent behavior.

where he was arrested the next day after a traffic stop. The US Justice Department immediately began investigating his crime as a hate crime—a crime motivated by the perpetrator's hatred toward a particular category of people—because of Roof's racist statements. In July 2015, a federal grand jury indicted Roof on hate crime charges. He also faced state criminal charges for murder. The federal government pursued the hate crime charges under federal laws because South Carolina has no specific hate crime statute.

WHO WERE ROOF'S VICTIMS?

Roof killed nine people. The Reverend Clementa Pinckney, 41, was the senior pastor at Emanuel AME Church and also served as a state senator. Cynthia Hurd, 54, had worked for the Charleston County Public Library for 31 years. The Reverend Sharonda Coleman-Singleton, 45, was a pastor at Emanuel. Tywanza Sanders, 26, had graduated from Allen University in Columbia, South Carolina, in 2014 with a degree in business administration. Ethel Lance, 70, had attended Emanuel Church most of her life. She worked as a custodian and was a mother and grandmother. Susie Jackson, 87, was Lance's cousin and was also a longtime church member. Depayne Middleton Doctor, 49, sang in the church choir. The Reverend Daniel Simmons, 74, was previously a pastor at another church. He survived the initial shooting but died in surgery. Myra Thompson, 59, was married to the Reverend Anthony Thompson of the Holy Trinity Reformed Episcopal Church.

After the shootings, the public began learning about Roof's beliefs and persona. His online manifesto and Facebook page were widely viewed. One Facebook photo

Roof appeared at a court hearing in July 2015.

showed him wearing a jacket with patches depicting old flags that represented racist regimes in Africa. Another photo showed him with a Confederate flag. While some people view this flag as a part of Southern heritage, many see it as a symbol tied to a history of slavery and discrimination.

But victims' families and the community did not allow Roof to stir up hatred. Family members addressed him directly via video feed during his first court appearance.

They made it clear they forgave him for what he did. "We welcomed you Wednesday night in our Bible study with open arms. We enjoyed you, but may God have mercy on your soul," stated Felicia Sanders, mother of victim Tywanza Sanders, 26.[4] Nadine Collier, daughter of victim Ethel Lance, told Roof, "You hurt me. You hurt a lot of people, but God forgives you, and I forgive you."[5] And Alana Simmons, granddaughter of victim Reverend Daniel Simmons, said, "Hate won't win."[6]

Charleston mayor Joe Riley also spoke about defying Roof's aspirations, noting that Roof "had this crazy idea that he would divide us. All this did was make us more united and love each other even more."[7]

ROOF'S RACIST MANIFESTO

Roof displayed his manifesto online. In this document, he explained his reasons for planning his attack. He stated that he was not raised in a racist home. In the schools he attended, he wrote, white and black kids traded racist jokes, but there was little animosity. "The event that truly awakened me was the Trayvon Martin case," he explained. What angered Roof was that the incident received nonstop publicity. Roof described black people as stupid and violent, writing, "Segregation did not exist to hold back negroes. It existed to protect us from them." He then stated that someone had to stop blacks from taking over America. He chose Charleston for his deed "because it is the most historic city in my state."[8]

QUESTIONS ABOUT RACISM

However, not everyone agreed with Riley's assessment.

Many noted South Carolina's racist past was still thriving, as evidenced by the fact that the Confederate flag still flew on the South Carolina statehouse grounds. Indeed, the fact that Roof targeted his victims based on their race led Charleston and the entire nation to reexamine the reality of racism in society. "Charleston has been transformed by tragedy into a ground zero for the racial strife reignited in recent years by a call of 'black lives matter,'" stated an article in the Charleston newspaper *The Post and Courier*.[9]

> "[ROOF] WAS LOOKING FOR THE TYPE OF CHURCH AND THE TYPE OF PARISHIONERS WHOSE DEATH WOULD IN FACT DRAW GREAT NOTORIETY FOR . . . HIS RACIST VIEWS."[10]
>
> **—US ATTORNEY GENERAL LORETTA LYNCH**

An organization called Black Lives Matter grew out of protests after black teenager Trayvon Martin was shot by George Zimmerman in 2012 in Florida. It gained traction after several police shootings of African Americans over the next few years. The movement argues racism and unfair treatment of blacks are deeply entrenched in US society, and that this leads to racially motivated hate crimes. Others believe racist individuals, not institutional racism, are ultimately responsible for hate crimes.

After the Charleston shootings, bouquets of flowers with heartfelt messages poured in from all over the United States. Thousands of people visited Emanuel AME Church to pay their respects. Visitors cried with local residents as they all wrote on a commemorative banner. And the shootings led to a major decision by the South Carolina legislature in July 2015. Legislators voted to remove the Confederate flag from the statehouse grounds and relocate it to a military museum. Governor Nikki Haley, who supported the removal, stated, "No one should drive by the statehouse and feel pain, no one should ever drive by the statehouse and feel like they don't belong."[11] But despite the feelings of unity in the aftermath of the events of June 17, 2015, hate crimes continue to occur in America.

FROM THE HEADLINES

IS RACISM ALIVE AND WELL?

The Charleston shootings awakened much debate about racism in the United States. An editorial in the *Wall Street Journal* argued institutional racism has vanished, while admitting that some individuals hold racist views. The editorial contrasted the Charleston shootings to the 1963 bombing of an African-American church in Birmingham, Alabama, that killed four girls and injured many. It stated, "Back then and before, the institutions of government—police, courts, organized segregation—often worked to protect perpetrators of racially motivated violence, rather than their victims. . . . Today the system and philosophy of institutionalized racism . . . no longer exists."[12]

The Black Lives Matter organization holds the opposing viewpoint. It describes itself as "an ideological and political intervention in a world where Black lives are systematically and intentionally targeted for demise."[13] Black Lives Matter supporters have held protests and demonstrations to spread this view, often focusing on cases in which police officers have shot African Americans.

The Black Lives Matter organization is one of today's largest and best-known antiracism movements.

CHAPTER TWO

WHAT ARE
HATE CRIMES?

Hate crimes are crimes motivated by prejudice against people based on race, religion, ethnicity, gender, sexual orientation, disability, or other factors. The perpetrator is biased against the victim. For this reason, hate crimes are sometimes known as bias crimes. The term *hate crime* was not used until the mid-1980s, but bias-motivated crimes have occurred throughout human history. These crimes may involve harassment, assault, murder, arson, vandalism, or verbal threats.

In November 2015, the Federal Bureau of Investigation (FBI) reported 5,479 hate crimes occurred in the United States in 2014.[1] However, many hate crimes are not reported. Experts estimate the true number of

Hate crimes differ from ordinary crimes in the specific, biased motivations of the perpetrators.

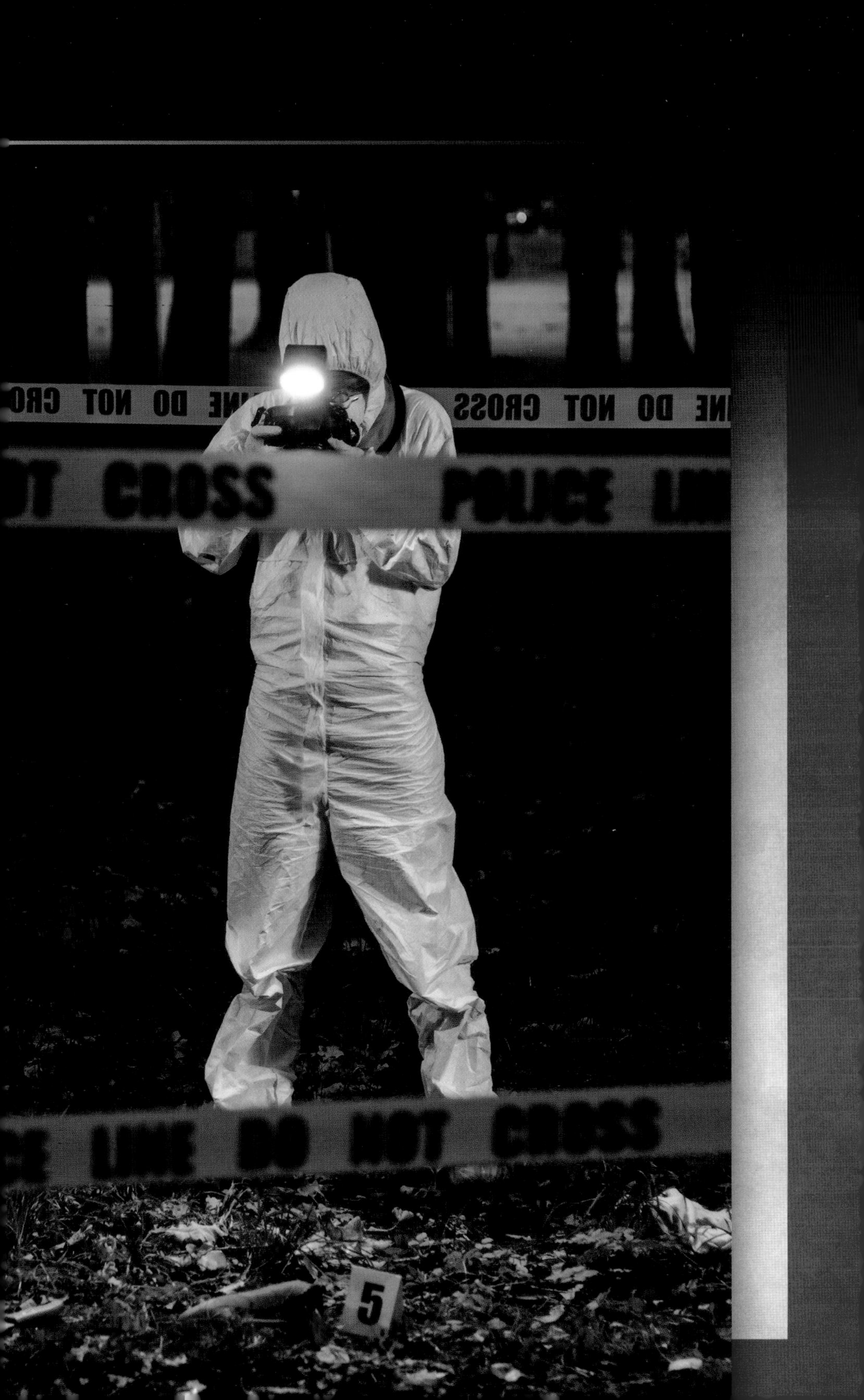

DO NOT CROSS
CROSS POLICE
LINE DO NOT CROSS
5

annual hate crimes to be approximately 260,000.[2] A June
2016 Associated Press investigation found more than 2,700
city police departments and county sheriff's departments
did not report any hate crimes to the FBI between 2009
and 2015.[3] Civil rights advocates are concerned about
this fact. As the Reverend Raphael Warnock of Atlanta,
Georgia's Ebenezer Baptist Church stated, "without a
diagnosis, we don't know how serious the illness is. And without a diagnosis, there is no prescription."[4]

VANDALISM HATE CRIMES

Hate crimes that involve property damage impact the targeted category by making its members feel vulnerable. In one such crime, William Blackford kicked and shattered the glass door at a gas station belonging to Omar and Adel Mohamed in Louisiana. Blackford told police he targeted the Muslim owners, saying, "We need to get them out of our country."[5]

However, in some crimes, the intent of the perpetrator is not clear. In April 2016, Christian Roberts of Midvale, Utah, reported that an unknown person burned a gay pride flag Roberts had hanging in his yard. Roberts said, "It was deliberate, someone wants to send a message."[6] But police emphasized there was as yet no proof of a hate crime.

DESCRIBING HATE CRIMES

Although prejudice or hatred
trigger hate crimes, these
opinions and emotions are
not crimes themselves. A
criminal action must result
from them to qualify as a hate
crime. There must be evidence
the perpetrator targeted the

victim based on his or her animosity toward the category the victim represents. According to hate-crime expert Brian Levin, proving such a motive is difficult because "getting into their mindset as to why they did it can be shrouded, particularly if the defendant doesn't have any overt communication [or say something] with regard to his motive."[7]

In their book *Hate Crimes Revisited*, experts Jack McDevitt and Jack Levin detail resentment, one common motivator for these crimes. Perpetrators may feel as though they are being victimized by society, and in searching for someone to blame, they lash out at whatever category of people they feel is responsible. A decline in the economic welfare among many middle-class Americans over the past several decades has helped spur such feelings, especially when they feel other categories of people are competing for jobs or wealth. Historically, feelings of hatred or resentment have also been reactions to wider world events. During World War II (1939–1945), Americans of Asian descent were targeted because the United States was at war with Japan. And after the terror attacks of September 11, 2001, Americans of Arab descent

were targeted because the attackers were from the Middle East.

To prosecute a hate crime, there must be evidence of the perpetrator's bias. Things said by the perpetrator during the crime, such as racial or religious epithets, are one example of evidence. Another example might be the fact that a perpetrator has carried out multiple attacks against the same category of people. If the perpetrator belongs to a recognized hate group, this might serve as additional evidence.

Another term used to describe hate crimes is *ethnoviolence*. Sociologist Howard Ehrlich, director of the Prejudice Institute, coined this term in 1986. Ehrlich believes ethnoviolence includes criminal acts, such as assault, and psychological abuse, such as taunting, based on prejudice. Both physical and psychological assaults, he states, are devastating to the victim. Using the term *ethnoviolence* makes the public aware of these effects, even if an act is not an actual crime.

Discrimination during World War II led to the imprisonment of many Japanese Americans in the United States.

ANATOMY OF A HATE GROUP

The Ku Klux Klan has intimidated, maimed, and murdered hundreds of Jews and people of color since its founding in 1865. The white robes and hoods worn by KKK members have become a symbol of terror and intimidation. However, in trying to retain members and recruit new ones, the organization has attempted to take its racist ideology into the mainstream in recent years. Some groups have barred explicitly violent people from meetings, while others have begun describing themselves as "lov[ing] the White race" rather than hating others.[9] In 2015, there were 190 Ku Klux Klan groups in the United States.

INDIVIDUALS AND HATE GROUPS

People of all ages, races, and ethnicities commit hate crimes. However, perpetrators are most likely to be young white males. These perpetrators can act independently, as part of informal groups, or with organized hate groups. "All hate groups have beliefs or practices that attack or malign an entire class of people, typically for their immutable characteristics," explains the Southern Poverty Law Center (SPLC), which tracks hate groups in America. The SPLC counted 457 hate groups in the United States in 1999. That number rose steadily and peaked at 1,018 in 2011. In 2015, there were 892 tracked hate groups.[8] Many of these groups, such as the Ku Klux Klan (KKK), target multiple categories of victims.

Some may assume organized hate groups commit most hate crimes. However, individuals or informal groups of friends are more often responsible. For example, on June 26, 2011, 18-year-old Deryl Dedmon was with nine other white teenagers at a party in Rankin County, Mississippi. The group piled into Dedmon's pickup and one other truck. They drove to nearby Jackson, which they called Jafrica. The teens saw 49-year-old James Anderson, a black man, in a parking lot near the freeway. They beat him and yelled racial slurs. Then Dedmon got back into his truck. He floored the gas and ran over Anderson, killing him instantly. No one tried to stop Dedmon. A nearby surveillance camera documented the entire event. In 2015, the participants were all convicted of a hate crime.

HATE CRIME VICTIMS

Hate crimes range from acts such as spitting at, threatening, or hitting an individual to torture and murder. The less extreme crimes rarely receive much media coverage, but they are still classified as hate crimes. For example, in December 2015, a black man pushed and then punched a Jewish man in the face and stomach at Medgar

The intentional destruction of religious texts, such as Islam's Koran, can be a hate crime.

Evers College in Brooklyn, New York. When asked why he did it, he allegedly said, "I don't like white and Jewish. Leave the school, you Jew."[10]

Hate crimes may also be directed against institutions or symbols associated with a particular group, such as churches, community centers, crosses, or cemeteries. The FBI's 2015 report revealed 36.1 percent of hate crimes were against property, while 63.1 percent were against people. Perpetrators targeted people or property based on race in 47 percent of these crimes. They targeted 18.6 percent based on religion, 18.6 percent for sexual orientation, 11.9 percent for ethnicity, 1.8 percent for gender identity, 1.5 percent for disability, and 0.6 percent for gender.[11]

EFFECTS OF HATE CRIMES

Hate crimes have personal, emotional, social, economic, and cultural costs. On a personal level, victims of hate crimes are frequently more traumatized than victims of crimes that do not involve bias. This is partly because they are typically beaten or otherwise assaulted more viciously than other crime victims are. Hate crime victims are usually hospitalized longer than victims of other crimes as well. This prolongs the physical and emotional trauma. In addition, people who belong to more than one frequently targeted group, such as a person who is both gay and African American, also tend to experience more violent crimes than others.

Common victim reactions include anger, fear, nonstop thinking about the event, social withdrawal, and thoughts of revenge. Many victims also experience sleeplessness, difficulties functioning at work or school, and alcohol and drug abuse. One reason these effects are so severe is that people are usually victimized for qualities they cannot change. People can do things such as installing burglar alarms to prevent home invasions. They cannot, however, change their race or ethnicity. Legal scholar Frederick M. Lawrence thus describes hate crimes as "an attack from which there is no escape."[12]

Levin and McDevitt, in describing the terrorist attacks of September 11, 2001, as a hate crime against Americans, note that the incident highlights this characteristic of hate crimes. The random nature of the attack made all Americans feel uneasy, as though no matter what

TERRORISM OR HATE CRIME?

Confusion exists about whether events such as the Charleston, South Carolina, shootings are hate crimes or terrorism. Indeed, the FBI debated whether to charge Roof with domestic terrorism or a hate crime. By definition, both acts seek to intimidate others and convey an ideological or political statement. Usually, prosecutors charge suspects with ties to terrorist groups outside the United States with terrorism. Those who use bombs, rather than guns alone, are also likely to be called terrorists.

they did, there was a chance they could be at risk from another such attack. And because the attack was random, there was no telling where the next one would happen. Anyone in the targeted category of people—in this case, Americans—would feel in potential danger at all times. Any hate crime can cause the same psychological effect on affected communities.

Lawrence notes that since a bias crime "attacks the victim not only physically but at the very core of his identity," this also makes others in the victim's category feel vulnerable.[13] Writer Andrew Sullivan expressed this phenomenon after the murder of a gay man, Matthew Shepard, in 1998. "I think a lot of gay people, when they first heard of that horrifying event, felt sort of punched in the stomach. I mean it kind of encapsulated all our fears of being victimized," he stated.[14] This wider impact is one reason many experts consider hate crimes to be worse than other crimes.

CHAPTER THREE

WHY DO
HATE CRIMES
OCCUR?

People commit hate crimes for a variety of reasons. These include anger, hatred, frustration, prejudice, poor judgement, mental illness, and political and religious beliefs. In turn, these motivating emotions or opinions may result from personal experiences or learned behaviors. Any of these factors can lead individuals to resent people who are different from themselves.

Often, people in dominant cultural groups, such as heterosexual white males, commit hate crimes because they view their targets as inferior, frightening,

Ideologies centered around hatred, such as white supremacy, are often linked to hate crimes.

or threatening to their political or economic power and status. But anyone of any race or social status may lash out when they feel threatened. This often happens when economic downturns leave people unemployed or impoverished. They may blame religious minorities, immigrants, or other categories of people for their misfortunes.

FEARS AND THREATS

The number of hate crimes against Latino and Asian immigrants has increased in recent years for economic and other reasons. One reason may involve projections that whites will be outnumbered by other races in the United States by 2050. Some white people view this as a threat to their power and status. "Being 'American' still means, in the minds of many people . . . being white," writes sociologist Joe Feagin.[1] Feagin asserts that the desire to preserve what some view as the traditional American culture can cause "a defensive response" that takes on the form of racism and hate crimes.[2]

Such acts have also been fueled by controversies about undocumented, or illegal, immigrants in the United States.

Resentment has led to crimes such as the beating of Latino immigrants as a sport. This practice became newsworthy after seven teens in Patchogue, New York, killed Marcelo Lucero in 2008. In many less severe assaults, the perpetrators did not fear detection. They knew the fear of deportation would prevent most undocumented immigrants from reporting the crimes.

Other hate crimes reflect Americans' fear of terrorists. Hate crimes against Muslims have increased since the terror attacks on September 11, 2001, and subsequent incidents. For instance, a man who yelled, "I'm gonna kill Muslims!" beat up Sarker Haque in New York after the terror attacks of December 2, 2015, in San Bernardino, California.[3] In another December 2015 incident, Denise Slader tossed coffee at Rasheed Albeshari

HATE CRIMES AGAINST ASIAN AMERICANS

Attorney Terri Yuh-lin Chen is an expert on hate crimes against Asian Americans. Chen notes hate crimes against Asian immigrants in the 1800s were motivated by the perception they were stealing jobs from Americans. But in modern times, "most hate crimes committed against Asian Americans draw upon notions of Asian Americans as perpetual foreigners who do not belong in this society," Chen writes. In other words, some Americans think of Asian Americans as outsiders because of their race, whether or not they are citizens. "Hate crimes against Asian Americans take on the unique dimension of operating as a form of border patrol and protection of the nation against the foreign 'alien,'" she adds.[4]

In February 2015, Muslim women prayed outside the White House in memory of three Muslims murdered in North Carolina.

in a San Francisco, California, park. Slader said she lashed out because Islam is "of the devil."[5] Many who target Muslims believe the religion is a threat because some of its most radical adherents advocate terrorism, despite the fact that such extremists make up only a minuscule percentage of the world's 1.6 billion Muslims.

Some religion-based hate crimes result from historical animosity between groups rather than from events such as terrorism. For example, hate crimes carried out by Muslims against Jews have increased in the United States in the early 2000s. Tensions in the Middle East between Israel and its largely Muslim neighbors likely contribute to this. A 2015 report by the Simon Wiesenthal Center revealed 54 percent of Jewish students on US college campuses had experienced or witnessed bias assaults and threats.[6] Muslims were perpetrators in many of these incidents. Other crimes have targeted Jewish institutions. In one case, Naveed Haq was sentenced to life in prison in 2010 for killing Pamela Waechter and injuring five others at the Jewish Federation of Greater Seattle on July 28, 2006. During his rampage, Haq screamed about his hatred for Jews and Israel.

"NAVEED HAQ'S INTENTION WAS TO FRIGHTEN JEWS EVERYWHERE AND INSTILL FEAR THAT THEY COULD BE THE NEXT CONVENIENT TARGET."[7]

—PROSECUTOR DAN SATTERBERG, AFTER HAQ'S CONVICTION

THEORIES ABOUT WHY HATE CRIMES OCCUR

Psychologists and sociologists have proposed several theories to explain how and why these biases and criminal behaviors occur. One group of theories includes what are known as social-learning theories. Their central idea is that people—especially children—internalize the ideas they are exposed to at home and in schools, churches, and other settings. When these ideas include prejudice, biased acts can result.

GOVERNMENT ATTITUDES

Implied or explicit government support for prejudice and hate crimes can influence the public's willingness to commit and unwillingness to condemn these acts. Official government policy and hate crime laws in the 2000s condemn and aggressively prosecute such crimes. However, government officials and law enforcement agencies often ignored or promoted such acts in the past. Before and during the civil rights movement of the 1950s and 1960s, police often ignored mob lynchings of minorities. Leaders' statements also demonstrated prejudice. For example, President Theodore Roosevelt, who served from 1901 to 1909, publicly stated, "A perfectly stupid race can never rise to a very high plane. The negro, for instance, has been kept down as much by lack of intellectual development as by anything else."[9]

Another commonly internalized notion is that violence is an everyday occurrence. This includes violence within families, communities, and the world, as well as in movies and on television. "As violence is increasingly modeled in all dimensions of life, people have come to include a violent response as a behavioral option," Ehrlich writes.[8] Therefore, some people may see the use of violence to express an opinion as acceptable.

Former neo-Nazi T. J. Leyden is a notable example of how social learning occurs. Leyden's father and grandfather taught him racism was acceptable. In addition, the only time he received praise and affection from his father was when he was beating up other kids. As a teenager, he met older neo-Nazis who nurtured his violent tendencies. "The gang gave me everything I lacked—identity, purpose, a direction in life," he stated.[10] But he also proved that learned ideas can be unlearned. Leyden renounced the white supremacist movement after realizing he was teaching his own children to hate.

DEPERSONALIZATION

Researchers have proposed that another type of social learning stems from the depersonalization that pervades society. Depersonalization can occur when government institutions and other bureaucracies treat people like numbers and objects. Sociologists believe this makes it easier for people to attack others. "Violence becomes acceptable when the other person is objectified or depersonalized," Ehrlich writes.[11]

REJECTING PREJUDICE

Many times, those who commit hate crimes learn prejudice at home. But sometimes children of hate-group members renounce their upbringing. For example, Carolyn Wagner, the daughter of Klansman Edward Greenwood, found the Klan's activities reprehensible. As a teenager, her father made her drive him to meetings. She, like her mother, feared her father's violent tendencies and said nothing. However, in 1965, Wagner watched the group tie a black man to a tree and beat him with a bullwhip. They then tied him to nearby railroad tracks. After taking her father home, she went back and untied the man. Wagner later became a civil rights advocate and founded Families United Against Hate to help people affected by hate crimes. "I realized I can make a choice to be a passive observer or I can become involved to diminish the harm that they're doing," she told the SPLC.[13]

Depersonalization motivates many hate crime perpetrators to feel no remorse about their crimes. For example, on April 12, 2014, neo-Nazi Glenn Miller, also known as Glenn Cross, murdered three people in Overland Park, Kansas. Two of the murders occurred outside the Jewish Community Center of Greater Kansas City, and the third happened in the parking lot of the Village Shalom Retirement Center. During his trial in 2015, Miller said he was "floating on a cloud" since the killings. When the prosecutor told jurors that Miller wanted to kill as many people as possible, Miller said, "I wanted to kill Jews, not people."[12] The sad irony is, all three of Miller's victims were Christians.

MEDIA INFLUENCES

News reports, advertising, movies, video games, music, and other media also play a big role in influencing people's perceptions about which groups are desirable or undesirable. For instance, hate crime researcher Carolyn Turpin-Petrosino believes remarks by radio talk-show host Rush Limbaugh have fueled anti-Hispanic hostility. In one show, Limbaugh called undocumented immigrants an "invasive species."[14]

In a SPLC interview, T. J. Leyden shed light on another media source that influences people to join hate groups. "If I filled a room with 1,000 neo-Nazi Skinheads and asked them 'What's the single most important thing that influenced you to join the neo-Nazi Skinhead movement?' probably 900 of them would say the [neo-Nazi punk rock] music," he stated.[15]

OTHER THEORIES

Other theories center on how individuals become delinquents and how group conflicts develop. For instance, sociologist Travis Hirschi developed a social control theory. It states delinquency results from a lack

of social bonds. The theory begins with the assumption that people are naturally able to commit crimes, but social bonds and values usually prevent this from happening. Conversely, those who lack these bonds are more likely to break the law.

Realistic group conflict theory holds that hate crimes result from an us-versus-them mentality. Conflicts develop because in-groups, or dominant groups, believe out-groups threaten their survival by competing for limited resources such as jobs, food, and money. This theory helps explain why hate crimes often occur when new immigrants compete with longtime citizens for jobs. A closely related theory is strain theory. This theory postulates people who are frustrated by not achieving their goals respond by lashing out and blaming others. No single theory explains or accounts for all the forces that drive prejudice and hate crimes. But together, these theories shed light on factors that contribute to these phenomena.

After leaving the white supremacist movement, Leyden turned his attention to advocating for tolerance and peace.

CHAPTER FOUR

THE HISTORY OF
HATE CRIMES IN AMERICA

P rejudice and hate crimes have existed throughout US history. In fact, many such crimes were encouraged or ignored by government officials for many years. These crimes were not legally distinguished from other crimes throughout much of American history. However, they clearly met the modern criteria for hate crimes.

In early US history, crimes that would be classified as hate crimes today were directed at Native Americans. White settlers backed by government officials and troops often kidnapped, robbed, enslaved, or murdered

Attacks on Native Americans date back to the earliest years of European settlement in the Americas.

HATE CRIMES AGAINST NATIVE AMERICANS

The US government and white settlers justified atrocities against Native Americans as necessary for America's westward expansion. However, history professor Gayle Olson-Raymer explains these actions also resulted from prejudice. European settlers, she writes, believed Native Americans were savages, and white Christians were their saviors. Olson-Raymer notes that Cotton Mather espoused such views when he wrote, "Probably the Devil' had delivered these 'miserable savages' to America 'in hopes that the gospel of the Lord Jesus Christ would never come here to destroy or disturb his absolute empire over them.'"[2] Such views can be traced back hundreds of years. In the 1200s, Olson-Raymer writes, Pope Innocent IV proclaimed "Europeans had a divine mandate to protect the spiritual well-being of all people."[3]

Native Americans. These actions often resulted from resentment over Native American tribes fighting to keep the tribal lands taken by white settlers.

Government officials targeted many tribes for extermination. In 1851, for example, California governor Peter Burnett declared "A war of extermination will continue to be waged . . . until the Indian race becomes extinct."[1] Laws that allowed forced enslavement of Native Americans, including children, were also enacted nationwide. Some local and federal government officials found these actions troubling, but they rarely intervened. Most believed these actions were necessary for American political and social progress.

THE SLAVERY ERA AND LYNCH MOBS

Many American colonists viewed the Africans they began enslaving in the 1600s as similar to Native Americans— uncivilized, evil, and inferior. According to the National Park Service Ethnography Program,

"ESTABLISHED IN THE MIDST OF ANOTHER AND A SUPERIOR RACE, AND WITHOUT APPRECIATING THE CAUSES OF THEIR INFERIORITY OR SEEKING TO CONTROL THEM, THEY MUST NECESSARILY YIELD TO THE FORCE OF CIRCUMSTANCE AND ERE LONG DISAPPEAR."[5]

—PRESIDENT ANDREW JACKSON, 1833 MESSAGE TO CONGRESS ABOUT NATIVE AMERICANS

"All of the colonies developed laws to establish and maintain dominance over African members of society."[4] These colonial laws evolved into the so-called Black Codes that regulated the activities of free and enslaved blacks until after the Civil War (1861–1865). The fact that society viewed blacks as inferior made it easy to accept the many biased acts committed against them.

One of the most violent types of crimes committed against blacks and others was lynching. Lynchings were a type of vigilante justice that involved a mob attacking someone they believed had violated a social norm or law. Lynchings became commonplace during the 1700s, 1800s, and early 1900s. Mobs often murdered victims for simply

The KKK and its intimidation tactics, such as cross burning, have been around for more than a century.

being impolite. Groups such as the KKK initiated many of these lynchings. Many lynchings involved cooperation or support from local police.

Lynch mobs commonly targeted blacks. However, Jews were also frequent targets. In one widely publicized case, Leo Frank, who was Jewish, was wrongly charged with murdering teenager Mary Phagan in Atlanta. Jury bias led

MORE TO THE
STORY

CHARLES LYNCH AND LYNCH LAW

Army officer Charles Lynch, who fought in the American Revolutionary War (1775–1793), organized his own court, outside the law, to decide the fate of accused criminals during the 1700s. Soon, the term *lynch law* was being used to refer to Lynch's methods of illegally administering punishment.

Police legitimized lynchings by participating in or ignoring them. For example, on June 20, 1921, a local state court convicted John Williams, who was black, of murdering a white girl in Moultrie, Georgia. Williams was scheduled to be executed on July 8. After the trial, 50 armed sheriffs escorted Williams to jail. A lynch mob of 500 people overwhelmed the sheriffs, who did not resist.[6] The mob tore off Williams's clothes, mutilated him, tied him to a tree stump, and set the stump on fire. Then, "A hundred men and women, old and young, grandmothers among them, joined hands and danced around while the Negro burned," according to an article in the *Washington Eagle*.[7]

> "WHEN THE POLICE ARRESTED A JEW, AND A YANKEE JEW AT THAT, ALL THE INBORN PREJUDICE AGAINST THE JEWS ROSE UP IN A FEELING OF SATISFACTION, THAT HERE WOULD BE A VICTIM WORTHY TO PAY FOR THE CRIME."[9]
>
> **—THE PASTOR OF THE CHURCH MARY PHAGAN, A 1913 ATLANTA MURDER VICTIM, ATTENDED**

to a death sentence for Frank despite the lack of evidence against him. Georgia's governor commuted the sentence to life in prison because of doubts about Frank's guilt. But a lynch mob took matters into their own hands on August 17, 1915. Twenty-five men entered the prison, beat up the guards, dragged Frank from his cell, and hung him from a tree.[8]

RESENTMENT AGAINST NEWCOMERS

In the 1800s, resentment and hate crimes were also directed against new immigrants. For example, many Asian laborers came to the United States to work on major projects such as the railroads. Many whites viewed Asians as inferior and blamed them for stealing jobs. The US government enacted anti-Asian laws. For example, in 1882, Congress passed the Chinese Exclusion Act. This law prohibited Chinese laborers from immigrating to the

United States and restricted the ability of workers already in the United States to become citizens.

Some violence was directed against religious groups, such as the members of the Church of Jesus Christ of Latter-day Saints, or the Mormons. On October 30, 1838, for instance, local militiamen attacked a Mormon community in Missouri after Missouri's governor issued an extermination order against Mormons. The order was based on the perception that Mormons represented a public threat.

AFTER THE CIVIL WAR

After the American Civil War ended, the freeing of slaves led a group of Southerners to form the Ku Klux Klan to fight against legislation that recognized blacks as citizens with equal rights. The KKK went on to target other groups, such as Jews, Roman Catholics, and Asians, with acts of intimidation, aggression, and murder. Membership in the Klan skyrocketed nationwide during the late 1800s and early 1900s.

Violence against African Americans became more prevalent outside the South as many Southern blacks

NEIGHBORHOOD PREJUDICE

Hundreds of thousands of African Americans who migrated northward, eastward, and westward from the South after the Civil War contributed to overcrowding in cities nationwide. Established black and white residents thus resented the newcomers. White residents in particular fought to keep blacks out of their neighborhoods. They harassed potential home buyers and renters and created property associations with restrictive rules to keep blacks out. For example, the Kenwood and Hyde Park Property Owner's Association in Chicago formed in the early 1900s to stop the so-called "Negro invasion."[10] According to the association's newsletter, this was important because blacks reportedly became dangerous when allowed to mix with whites. Such racist attitudes contributed to many acts of vandalism and assault that led to the 1918 Chicago race riots.

moved northward, starting in the 1890s. Many longtime residents of Northern cities resented the arrival of African Americans. Intimidation and violence were especially prevalent in Chicago, Illinois; Detroit, Michigan; and New York City. This happened in the landmark *Ossian Sweet* case. The case involved a black doctor named Ossian Sweet moving into a white neighborhood in Detroit. Sweet, his family, and friends inside the house armed themselves for protection against a white mob on September 9, 1925. Gunshots killed a white man and wounded a white teenager. With help from the National Association for the Advancement of Colored People (NAACP), Sweet and his codefendants were not convicted of a crime.

A brief for the case noted, "While the North would claim the moral high ground when it came to race relations, they were not so tolerant when thousands of blacks migrated north to escape the worst forms of racism in the South."[11]

THE CIVIL RIGHTS ERA

The NAACP, formed in 1909 to promote civil rights for blacks, was one organization that facilitated the civil rights movement of the 1950s and 1960s. Activists including Martin Luther King Jr. also challenged and began conquering the institutionalized segregation and mistreatment of African Americans. King's famous "I Have a Dream" speech in 1963 helped pave the way for groundbreaking civil rights legislation. In 1968, avowed

THE *OSSIAN SWEET* CASE

On September 9, 1925, approximately 400 white people surrounded the house Ossian Sweet had bought in Detroit.[12] The mob threw bricks and rocks and yelled racial slurs. The Sweets and friends inside the house knew other black families had experienced similar attacks. So they were well armed. Police who arrived did nothing to stop the mob. Then, gunshots fired from inside the house killed a white man and wounded a white teenager. The police arrested everyone inside the house.

The NAACP persuaded famed lawyer Clarence Darrow to defend Sweet and the others. Darrow used an innovative strategy. He put Ossian on the stand to describe how racist incidents throughout his life instilled intense fear. Darrow convinced an all-white jury the Sweets had the right to defend themselves and their property. The jury acquitted the defendants in a major step for civil rights.

The home of Ossian Sweet is now preserved as a historic landmark.

racist and anti-integrationist James Earl Ray assassinated

King in Memphis, Tennessee. Ray was imprisoned for life.

With the new civil rights laws came a reactionary

resurgence of the KKK and neo-Nazi groups to fight

mandatory desegregation. The KKK expressed its

opposition with bombings, church burnings, and murders.

"Its members enjoyed what initially amounted to general

immunity from arrest, prosecution and conviction. Many

police officers were members," history professor and

noted Klan scholar David Chalmers explains.[13] In the next

few decades, the legal efforts of anti-Klan activists led to the seizure of the group's property and the conviction of some of its members for murder, decades after the crimes took place. Though the Klan continued to exist in small, scattered groups, it was significantly weakened.

OLD AND NEW TARGETS

In the late 1900s and early 2000s, the influx of immigrants from non-English-speaking countries created new targets for hate crimes. Mexicans, Filipinos, and Indians were among them. At the same time, some groups that were historically attacked, such as blacks and Jews, were still targeted, while others, such as Catholics, became less frequent targets.

Other changes involve the use of the Internet to plan and execute hate crimes. Hate groups use the Internet to recruit new members and communicate with like-minded individuals and groups worldwide. What has not changed is that bias crimes continue to have damaging effects on individuals and society. Just as they did in early US history, these crimes continue to play a huge role in shaping social and legal policies.

THE EVOLUTION
OF HATE
CRIME LAWS

Modern US hate crime laws grew out of laws and policies established after slavery ended. The post-slavery laws attempted to address hate crimes against blacks and the damage done by slavery. The Civil Rights Act of 1866 made anyone born in the United States, including former slaves, a citizen. It also prescribed fines or jail sentences for anyone who interfered with any African American who was exercising civil rights. The Fourteenth Amendment to the Constitution, passed in 1868, reaffirmed the Civil Rights Act of 1866. It also prohibited states from

Lawmakers grappled with protecting the rights of millions of newly freed blacks following the Civil War.

depriving any person of life, liberty, or property without due process of law. The Fifteenth Amendment, passed in 1870, gave all male citizens the right to vote.

Despite these new laws, the KKK, police, and Southern lawmakers routinely harassed and committed violent acts against blacks and other minorities. The federal government passed other new laws to address these abuses. The Force Act of 1870 and the Civil Rights Act of 1871, also known as the Ku Klux Klan Act, spelled out penalties for anyone who interfered with any citizen's civil rights. The 1871 law also prohibited wearing disguises under certain conditions and committing acts of terror in groups. It was clearly aimed at KKK activities. The 1871 law was the first law to criminalize bias-motivated crimes. According to Turpin-Petrosino, "The criminalization of that

TARGETING THE KKK

One section of the Civil Rights Act of 1871 was clearly aimed at the KKK's routine practice of terrorizing others in groups while concealed in white robes and hoods. Numerous US states also passed anti-mask laws directed at the Klan. For example, Georgia's 1951 Anti-Mask Law was enacted "in response to a demonstrated need to safeguard the people of Georgia from terrorization by masked vigilantes" and because "a nameless, faceless figure strikes terror in the human heart."[1]

which used to be a cultural norm [was] a monumental step."[2]

CIVIL RIGHTS LAWS

Even with the post-slavery laws, discriminatory practices and violence continued. However, several states did pass anti-lynch laws in the early 1900s. One of the first such laws was the 1921 Capehart Anti-Lynching Law in West Virginia. It made lynching a felony and subjected perpetrators to fines, jail time, and payment of financial restitution to victims' families. However, nearly 200 efforts to pass federal anti-lynch laws did not succeed.[3] Southern senators prevented Congress from passing these laws.

"WEST VIRGINIA WAS AHEAD OF THE CURVE WHEN THE STATE LEGISLATURE PASSED THE CAPEHART ANTI-LYNCHING LAW IN 1921."[4]

—HISTORY PROFESSOR TIM KONHAUS

Other practices, such as discriminatory state laws and the harassment of blacks who tried to vote, were exposed and addressed at the federal level during the civil rights movement. The Civil Rights Act of 1964 specifically addressed discrimination by prohibiting state and local governments from limiting access to public places, including hotels, theaters, and restaurants, based on race, religion, gender, or ethnicity. This law also gave the federal government the authority to prosecute some hate-motivated crimes. The first case prosecuted under this law was the murder of Lemuel Penn, a black man, on July 11, 1964, in Georgia. The federal government stepped in after a local jury did not convict the shooters.

Other laws, including the Civil Rights Act of 1968, the Fair Housing Act, the Civil Rights Restoration Act of 1988, and the Civil Rights Act of 1991, further expressed the intention of the US government to oppose and prosecute bias-motivated acts. Modern hate crime laws grew directly out of these civil rights laws.

APPLYING THE 1964 CIVIL RIGHTS ACT

The first case in which the federal government applied the landmark 1964 Civil Rights Act was the murder of Lemuel Penn. Penn, who was black, was an assistant superintendent of education in Washington, DC, and a lieutenant colonel in the US Army Reserves. On July 11, 1964, four KKK members shot and killed him near Athens, Georgia, as he drove home from military duty with two fellow officers. The state of Georgia charged KKK members Cecil Myers and Joseph Sims with the murder, but an all-white jury found them not guilty on September 4, 1964. Federal authorities, however, retried the case. They charged Sims, Myers, and four other KKK members with conspiring to violate Penn's civil rights. The court found four of the defendants innocent. But it convicted Sims and Myers and sentenced them to ten years in prison.

In 1963, Alabama governor George Wallace, *left*, stood at the entrance of a University of Alabama building to physically block black students from entering.

RESPONSE TO CIVIL RIGHTS LAWS

The KKK and other white supremacist groups responded to the civil rights laws by committing more bias attacks to block minorities from exercising their civil rights. Southern legislators tried to use legal methods to block these laws and requirements for school integration. For instance, 82 representatives and 19 senators from Southern states signed the Southern Manifesto of 1956. This document encouraged Southerners to use lawful means of blocking the "chaos and confusion" that school desegregation would bring.[5] It was not enacted as a law.

To better measure the continued efforts to harass and attack minorities, civil

TRACKING HATE CRIMES

Federal hate crime laws require law enforcement agencies to track and report hate crimes. The main sources of hate crime statistics are the FBI's Uniform Crime Reporting (UCR) Program and the Bureau of Justice Statistics National Crime Victimization Survey (NCVS). UCR data comes from local and state law enforcement agencies. NCVS data comes from surveys that ask selected households about hate crime victimization experiences. But many victims do not report bias crimes, so the true numbers are higher than the reported ones.

In addition, the definition of a hate crime varies among US states and among individuals. Thus, UCR and NCVS statistics are very different. For example, UCR reported a yearly average of 7,926 hate crimes from 2000 to 2005. NCVS reported that 191,000 hate crimes occurred between July 2000 and December 2003, averaging out to approximately 55,000 per year.[6] The government acknowledges these statistics are only estimates.

rights organizations pressured Congress to pass the Hate Crimes Statistics Act of 1990. The bill that led to this act was introduced in Congress by lawmakers John Conyers, Barbara Kennelly, and Mario Biaggi in 1985. They coined and first used the term *hate crime* in their bill. The bill required the US attorney general to collect and publish data on hate crimes, based on state government reports of acts motivated by bias against victims' race, religion, or ethnicity.

The 1990 law spurred many US states to start enacting their own hate crime laws. Before the law was passed, few states or localities documented or collected hate crime statistics, so little was known about how common these crimes were. However, many legal challenges to these laws led the Anti-Defamation League (ADL) to develop its Model Hate Crime Statute. This model contains elements that, based on the history of court cases dealing with hate crimes, are likely to withstand legal challenges. Many states have used the model to develop effective, lasting hate crime laws. By 2016, Wyoming, Georgia, Arkansas, South Carolina, and Indiana were the only states with no hate crime statutes.

THE 2009 HATE CRIMES PREVENTION ACT

On October 6, 1998, 21-year-old Matthew Shepard of Wyoming was beaten. His attackers, Aaron McKinney and Russell Henderson, both 21, used a .357 Magnum handgun.

The three men had been in a bar drinking, and Shepard had asked for a ride home. McKinney and Henderson left Shepard tied to a fence to die on a country road near Laramie, Wyoming. The following evening, mountain biker Aaron Kreifels found Shepard, who was unconscious and mutilated so badly that Kreifels thought he was a scarecrow. Shepard died five days later in Poudre Valley Hospital in Fort Collins, Colorado. The grisly crime was immediately labeled a hate crime because Shepard was gay.

THE ANTI-DEFAMATION LEAGUE'S MODEL HATE CRIME STATUTE

The Anti-Defamation League's Model Hate Crime Statute recommends that hate crime laws contain five elements. First, the law should specify that a hate crime includes an underlying crime and bias toward the victim because of his or her status in a particular category. Second, it should contain a penalty enhancement clause. This means penalties for a hate crime are more severe than penalties for the same crime without the bias element. Third, the law should spell out penalties for institutional vandalism, damaging buildings or other category-related symbols such as crosses. Fourth, it should include a civil action available for victims. This means the victim can sue the perpetrator for money, in addition to the state prosecuting the perpetrator for breaking the law. Fifth, it should mandate that the state will gather and report local hate crime statistics.

The murder of Matthew Shepard was among several catalysts for new laws dealing with hate crimes.

Matthew Shepard
1976–1998

Peace

It sparked worldwide outrage and calls for stronger federal hate crime statutes.

That same year, the brutal murder of James Byrd Jr., a black man, in Texas led to equally vehement protests against hate crimes. Three white men stopped and offered Byrd a ride while he was walking home. They took him to an isolated area and beat him. Then they chained him to their pickup truck and dragged him for several miles. They dumped his body near an African-American cemetery.

Neither murder could be tried as a hate crime because neither Wyoming nor Texas had hate crime laws. The federal government could not prosecute the cases as hate crimes either. This was because existing federal laws restricted federal intervention to acts such as voting, which were federally protected. Thus, although people referred to the acts as hate crimes, the perpetrators were not charged with committing hate crimes.

On October 28, 2009, President Barack Obama signed the Matthew Shepard and James Byrd Jr. Hate Crimes Prevention Act (HCPA) into law. The HCPA gives the federal government the authority to investigate and prosecute local hate crimes, with or without help from state or local prosecutors. It also allows hate crimes to be prosecuted in both federal and state courts when appropriate. The other main feature is that gender, sexual orientation, gender identity, and disability were added to the categories protected by hate crime laws. By 2016, the HCPA was the most recent federal hate crime law.

THE BIG DEBATE

It took Congress more than ten years to pass the Matthew Shepard and James Byrd Jr. Hate Crimes Prevention Act after activists began pushing for a new hate crime law. Many bills were proposed over the years in the House of Representatives and Senate. But debates about the need for and content of a new law derailed most efforts.

Remarks by congressmen and senators during these debates illustrate some of the arguments for and against hate crime laws. Congressman John Conyers of Michigan stated that such laws are needed because "these crimes of violence are directed not just at those who are directly attacked: they are targeting the entire group with the threat of violence."[7] In opposing the bill, Congressman Jason Chaffetz of Utah said, "This hate crimes bill says some Americans are more equal than others and deserve special treatment."[8]

CHAPTER SIX

THE NATURE OF MODERN HATE CRIME LAWS

U sually, state legislatures develop hate crimes laws, and hate crimes are prosecuted in state courts. But there are also federal hate crime laws, such as the HCPA, that give the federal government the power to get involved in some cases. Usually the federal government does so when a state lacks a hate crime law.

Hate crime laws differ from civil rights laws. Civil rights laws protect the rights of people to participate in activities that occur in public places. Hate crime laws protect individuals who are attacked because of bias

At the enactment of the HCPA, President Obama spoke alongside the families of Byrd and Shepard.

HATE CRIME LAWS AND THE FOURTEENTH AMENDMENT

The Fourteenth Amendment to the Constitution reads, in part, "No state shall . . . deny to any person within its jurisdiction the equal protection of the laws."[1] Some legal experts believe hate crime laws violate this equal protection clause by favoring selected people. But other experts argue these laws protect all people, not just minorities. "Because everyone has a race, religion, ethnicity, gender, and sexual orientation, hate crime laws protect everyone" who is targeted for any of these reasons, writes attorney Ave Mince-Didier.[2]

based on a variety of categories, including race, religion, ethnicity, and others.

ELEMENTS OF HATE CRIME LAWS

Most US states' hate crime laws are based on the Model Hate Crime Statute developed by the ADL. Such laws have withstood court challenges and are considered the most comprehensive hate crime laws. However, not all state laws contain all the elements the model recommends. These elements include specifics about protected categories of people, hate crime criteria, punishment, and data tracking. Different state laws also include different protected categories, criteria, and punishments.

For example, the majority of state laws include race, religion, national origin, and ethnicity as protected categories. Thirty-two state laws also include sexual orientation, 27 include gender, and 10 include gender identity.[3] The Iowa statute includes political affiliation. Forty-five state laws include penalty enhancements. This makes penalties for hate crimes more severe than for the same crime committed without a bias-driven motivation. The penalty enhancement clause in Wisconsin's hate crime law is typical of many such clauses. It reads, "If the crime committed . . . is ordinarily a class A misdemeanor, the penalty increase under this section changes the crime to a felony and the revised maximum fine is $10,000 and the revised maximum term of imprisonment is 2 years."[4]

CONTROVERSIES AND CHALLENGES

Controversies over certain elements of hate crime laws have led to court challenges. Two landmark cases that ultimately went to the US Supreme Court—*R.A.V. v. St. Paul* and *Wisconsin v. Mitchell*—ended up clearly defining which features are legal under the US Constitution.

R.A.V. v. St. Paul involved a 1990 crime in which Robert A. Viktora and several other teenagers burned a cross in the backyard of a black family. Viktora was charged under a Saint Paul, Minnesota, hate crime ordinance. However, a

Russell Jones and his wife, Laura, were the victims of Viktora's hate crime.

local court dismissed the charge on the grounds that the law interfered with his constitutional right to free speech. The prosecutors appealed, and the Minnesota Supreme Court overturned the local court's ruling. Viktora then appealed to the US Supreme Court. This court ruled the local court's original ruling was correct. The justices found the Saint Paul hate crime law was unconstitutional because "it prohibits otherwise permitted speech solely on the basis of the subjects the speech addresses."[5]

The US Supreme Court's 1993 decision in *Wisconsin v. Mitchell*, on the other hand, held that state laws that follow the Model Hate Crime Statute are constitutional.

It involved a dispute over penalty enhancements. This case evaluated whether Wisconsin's hate-crime penalty enhancement was legal. The defendant, Todd Mitchell, had urged a group of fellow black men to attack a 14-year-old white boy. Mitchell was angry about the movie *Mississippi Burning*, which depicted the murders of three civil rights workers in the 1960s. A local court convicted him of aggravated battery. He received an enhanced punishment of four years in prison because the crime involved racial bias. Mitchell appealed to the Wisconsin Supreme Court. He argued the penalty enhancement

HATE CRIME LAWS AND THE FIRST AMENDMENT

Because hate crimes can sometimes be identified based on something said by the perpetrator, such as a racial epithet, some legal experts believe hate crime laws violate the First Amendment to the Constitution. The First Amendment reads, in part, "Congress shall make no law . . . abridging the freedom of speech, or of the press."[6]

Numerous legal challenges to hate crime laws claim they infringe on free speech and punish ideas. But other experts note these laws punish behavior, not the ideas that trigger the behavior. ADL attorney Michael Lieberman explains these laws do not violate the First Amendment either: "The First Amendment does not protect violence, nor does it prevent the government from imposing criminal penalties for violent discriminatory conduct directed against victims on the basis of their personal characteristics."[7] The US Supreme Court agreed, finding in *Wisconsin v. Mitchell* that because crimes motivated by race or other categories have a severe impact on the victim and the community, the state of Wisconsin was able to use hate crime laws to discourage such crimes and attempt to prevent such an impact.

was unconstitutional. This court agreed with him, but prosecutors took the case to the US Supreme Court. The court ruled the penalty enhancement statute did not violate the Constitution because it punished behavior, not speech or opinion.

PENALTY ENHANCEMENTS

Congressman Jason Chaffetz expressed an argument against penalty enhancements: "It increases criminal penalties not based on the criminal act itself, but based on the thoughts and beliefs of the person who committed the act."[8] Chaffetz pointed out people's thoughts and beliefs cannot be punished. Only illegal acts are subject to punishment.

Supporters of penalty enhancements believe they are necessary because hate crimes impact entire categories of people. "Strong enforcement of these laws can have a deterrent impact and limit the potential for a hate crime incident to explode into a circle of violence," writes Wade Henderson, president of the Leadership Conference on Civil and Human Rights.[9]

MORE TO THE
STORY

IS PUNISHMENT ENHANCEMENT WARRANTED?

The US Supreme Court ruled in the *Wisconsin v. Mitchell* case that
hate-crime penalty enhancements are legal. The court based its
decision on three major arguments. First, the motive that underlies
other types of crimes is often considered in determining the
punishment. For example, someone who kills another in self-defense
may be punished less severely or not at all, compared with
someone who kills while robbing the victim. The second argument
is that hate crimes are more likely than other crimes to lead to
retaliation and emotional distress for people who share the victim's
race or other category. The court viewed this wider sphere of
ripple effects as warranting harsher punishment. Third, punishment
enhancements result from the perpetrator's acts, not ideas or
communications. They therefore do not violate the First Amendment.
Not all criminologists and legal experts agree with this ruling. Some
opponents believe a punishment should punish the criminal act,
regardless of the underlying bias or the effect of that bias on the
victim or the community.

Utah congressman Jason Chaffetz has criticized the basis of hate crime laws.

A NEW CONTROVERSY

A vote by the Louisiana state legislature on May 24, 2016, highlighted another controversy. Lawmakers voted to approve a so-called Blue Lives Matter bill that makes police officers and other first responders a protected category under hate crime laws. Louisiana governor John Bel Edwards signed the bill into law two days later. A crime against someone in a protected category can add five years to a prison sentence for a felony and six months to one year for a misdemeanor in Louisiana.

State Representative Lance Harris introduced the bill because he believes those who serve and protect others deserve extra protection. Harris noted police are often attacked "for no other reason than some people hate police. That's the definition of a hate crime."[10] However, the law has critics. The ADL, for instance, expressed its opposition because it believes it is inappropriate to make police and first responders a protected category. "ADL strongly believes that the list of personal characteristics included in hate crime laws should remain limited to immutable characteristics, those that can or should not be changed. Working in a profession is not a personal characteristic and is not immutable," stated an ADL press release.[11] ADL also believes adding more protected categories will "dilute" existing hate crime laws and make them less significant.[12] Ejike Obineme of the New Orleans Chapter of the Black Youth Project 100 had another objection to the new law.

"Including police as a protected class in hate crime legislation would serve to provide more protection to an institution that is statistically proven to be racist in action, policy and impact," he stated.[13]

"ADL IS CONCERNED THAT EXPANDING THE CHARACTERISTICS INCLUDED IN BIAS CRIME LAWS MAY OPEN THE DOOR TO A MYRIAD OF OTHER CATEGORIES TO BE ADDED AND SIMULTANEOUSLY DILUTE CURRENT HATE CRIMES LEGISLATION."[14]

—THE ANTI-DEFAMATION LEAGUE

CHAPTER SEVEN

ARE HATE
CRIME LAWS
NECESSARY?

There is much debate about whether hate crime laws are necessary. These debates center on questions about why or even whether hate crimes are different than or worse than other crimes.

ARGUMENTS IN FAVOR

One argument used in favor of hate crime laws is that hate crimes differ significantly in their impact from crimes that are not motivated by bias. The effect of hate crimes is to intimidate and instill fear in the victims. For example, in 2010, Ivaylo Ivanov of Brooklyn, New York, was sentenced to 18 years in prison for spray-painting

Proponents of hate crime laws argue that such crimes target and frighten entire communities, increasing their damaging effect.

swastikas and anti-Jewish slogans on synagogues and cars and for amassing an arsenal of weapons. He told police he committed these acts "knowing that said actions would cause annoyance and alarm."[1]

A closely related argument is that these crimes do not affect just victims and their families. Instead, the emotional effects impact entire communities. According to proponents of hate crime laws, this fact makes hate crimes worse and more damaging than other crimes. As attorney and hate crimes expert Frederick Lawrence explains, hate crimes represent "a deeper tear in the fabric of society."[2]

Some supporters of hate crime laws also argue that these laws demonstrate the government's commitment to respond to the historical isolation and victimization of racial minorities, gays, and other people. Brent Cox of the Matthew Shepard Foundation states that without a forceful response to hate crimes, affected people feel like "a group of second class citizens."[3]

ARGUMENTS AGAINST HATE CRIME LAWS

Many opponents of hate crime laws acknowledge that crimes motivated by bias and hatred occur. In their book

Hate Crimes: Criminal Law and Identity Politics, James Jacobs and Kimberly Potter describe hate crime laws as "well-intentioned" but argue there are several problems with them.[4] They believe identifying biased motivations is difficult and that selecting which categories to include in such laws will make people in excluded categories resentful. They also argue that incorporating into law the categorization of victims by race, religion, and other factors will serve to create wider divides in US culture. Jacobs and Potter write that hate crime laws provide yet another place for conflicts between people of different races, ethnicities, and religions.

Opponents of hate crime laws also believe these laws trigger animosity by inciting resentment over what they call "identity politics."[5] The phrase *identity politics* refers to ways in which people make political decisions based on their racial, sexual, or other identities. "Hate crime laws encourage

"THE NEW HATE CRIME LAWS EXTEND IDENTITY POLITICS TO THE DOMAIN OF CRIME AND PUNISHMENT. IN EFFECT, THEY REDEFINE THE CRIME PROBLEM AS YET ANOTHER ARENA FOR CONFLICT BETWEEN RACES, GENDERS, AND NATIONALITY GROUPS."[6]

—LAW PROFESSOR JAMES B. JACOBS AND LAWYER KIMBERLY POTTER

> "EVERY VIOLENT CRIME IS DEPLORABLE, REGARDLESS OF ITS MOTIVATION."[9]
>
> —US CONGRESSMAN LAMAR SMITH

IGNORING MOTIVATION

Opponents of hate crime laws believe the crime itself—not the perpetrator's motivations or the victim's identity—should determine the punishment. "Selectively protecting some while punishing others more severely based on their thoughts and beliefs is unequal, unjust, and un-American," said Congressman Jason Chaffetz.[10] Journalist Tish Durkin wrote in a *New York Times* opinion piece that hate crime laws "codify the idea that certain kinds of human life have greater value than other kinds."[11] But proponents of hate crime laws point out that hate crime laws protect categories of bias motivation, rather than select groups. In other words, rather than protecting specific groups, hate crime legislation protects everyone with a race, religion, or sexual orientation.

citizens to think of themselves as members of identity groups and encourage identity groups to think of themselves as victimized and besieged, thereby hardening each group's sense of resentment," write Jacobs and Potter.[7] The two scholars believe most laws, in contrast, unify society by uniformly "denouncing crime and the criminal" and reaffirming the government's "commitment to the society's core values and norms."[8]

PERCEPTION AND POLITICAL MOTIVES

Another argument against hate crime laws centers on findings that indicate the hate crime label depends more on

James Jacobs, *left*, argued against the need for hate crime laws at a 2012 congressional hearing.

76

Harpreet Saini

perceptions than reality. A closely related argument is that the government often uses the hate-crime label for political purposes. A 2011 case in Kentucky in which four members of the Jenkins family—David, Anthony, Alexis, and Ashley—kidnapped and assaulted Kevin Pennington, a gay man, illustrates these points. This was the first antigay case the federal government prosecuted under the HCPA.

All four family members were charged with a hate crime because Pennington, who escaped and ran away after being beaten, told police he was targeted because of his sexual orientation. Alexis and Ashley pleaded guilty and were sentenced to approximately eight years in prison. But David and Anthony's case went to trial. In 2012 a federal jury in London, Kentucky, convicted both men of kidnapping and

THE RARITY OF HATE CRIMES

Opponents of hate crime laws often argue these crimes are rare and thus do not deserve a separate status from ordinary crimes. The FBI reported 5,479 of the 9,443,214 crimes reported to law enforcement agencies in 2014 were classed as hate crimes.[12] However, Turpin-Petrosino argues against this viewpoint. "Terrorist acts are also rare, but because of the extraordinary ramifications of such acts, they are not only the subject of intense study but also the focus of special legislation and government policy," she writes.[13]

conspiracy, but acquitted them of a hate crime. Their attorneys had argued both were too intoxicated to plan or purposefully execute the attack. In addition, testimony from all four members of the Jenkins family convinced the jury the altercation resulted from a bad drug deal. Civil rights attorney AeJean Cha disputed this, saying, "This is not about drugs, this is about the fact that Kevin is gay."[14]

PRESSURE TO APPLY THE HATE CRIME LABEL

Opponents of hate crime laws argue these laws are often used as a political tool by special-interest groups and government officials. Special-interest groups may put pressure on police and public officials to demonstrate a commitment to fighting hate crimes. This pressure may lead police to rush to label a crime as a bias crime before the facts are known. Or it may result in angry special-interest groups denouncing police who do not conform to the group's demands. One example of this occurred in the case in which a group of men murdered Craig Cohen, a gay man, in Florida. Police began their investigation with the suspicion it was a hate crime. However, the investigation uncovered no such evidence. Some activists were reportedly upset at this and demanded a reinvestigation.

CHAPTER EIGHT

FREE SPEECH
AND HATE
SPEECH

Numerous hate-crime court cases have revolved around the First Amendment right of free speech. As hate crime expert Frederick Lawrence explains, "Free expression protects the right to express offensive views but not the right to behave criminally."[1]

In some instances, however, speech itself can be a criminal act. The government has the right to restrict and punish free speech when it encourages illegal behavior. Other acts of communication that are motivated by prejudice are legal if they do not directly threaten an individual or group and do not

Antigay protesters sometimes picket US soldiers' funerals, claiming the deaths are God's punishment for the country's acceptance of gay people. Such hateful speech is legal if it does not encourage violence.

violate local littering or trespassing laws. Protected acts include distributing hate-filled pamphlets and chanting hate slogans. Thus, speech such as that expressed by white supremacists at a 2008 rally in Jena, Louisiana, on Martin Luther King Jr. Day is legal. The group chanted, "If it ain't white, it ain't right."[2] But speech or symbols, such as swastikas or burning crosses, may be prohibited when used to intimidate. For example, on April 18, 2015, vandals in Rindge, New Hampshire, spray-painted swastikas and the word *Hitler* on a house where Jews lived. This was considered a hate crime because these are known symbols of violence against Jews.

IS IT THREATENING?

Sometimes it can be difficult to determine whether hate speech is intimidating or threatening. For example, in 2009, a South Carolina grocery store owner was arrested and charged with ethnic intimidation for remarks he believed were simply expressions of free speech.

"BIAS-TARGETED BEHAVIOR THAT IS INTENDED TO CREATE FEAR IN ITS TARGETED VICTIM IS A BIAS CRIME, WHETHER THE BEHAVIOR IS PRIMARILY VERBAL OR PHYSICAL."[3]

—ATTORNEY AND HATE CRIME EXPERT FREDERICK M. LAWRENCE

"You niggers are trespassing. Those people only come in a store to steal," he told a black couple who entered his store.[4] But then he threatened to kill the couple if they did not leave. The threat was what got him arrested.

In another example, in 2008, Bradley Smith of Modesto, California, was sentenced to six and one-half years in prison for repeatedly threatening Alfred Henderson and his family, who are black. Smith threatened to burn a cross on Henderson's property, abuse his wife, and bring KKK members to hang Henderson in a tree. The courts ruled Smith's threats constituted a hate crime because his intent was to frighten Henderson so much his family would move away—which they did.

> "SPEECH IS NOT CRIMINALIZED. THE CRIME IS TRIGGERED BY CONDUCT."[5]
>
> **—ADL ATTORNEY MICHAEL LIEBERMAN**

MURDER OR FREE SPEECH?

The case in which 18-year-old Tyler Clementi killed himself on September 22, 2010, also highlights differences between unprotected hate speech and free speech. Clementi was a gay student at Rutgers University.

His roommate, Dharun Ravi, secretly set up a webcam to spy on Clementi while Clementi was alone in their dorm room with another man. Ravi and his friend Molly Wei watched the video feed on Wei's computer. "I saw him making out with a dude. Yay," Ravi tweeted.[6] Ravi then invited his Twitter followers to a viewing party. Clementi became distraught after viewing Ravi's Twitter feed and finding out he was being ridiculed. He jumped off the George Washington Bridge two days later.

Many outraged people demanded Ravi be prosecuted for murder with penalty enhancements for a hate crime. However, others thought Ravi was just an arrogant teenager who should not be blamed for Clementi's death. Friends reported he was not homophobic. Ravi was not prosecuted for murder, but in 2012 was convicted of 15 crimes, including invasion of privacy and bias intimidation. He faced a maximum of ten years in jail but was sentenced to 30 days in jail, three years' probation, a $10,000 fine, community service, and mandatory counseling. In explaining why he did not impose a harsher sentence on Ravi, Judge Glenn Berman stated, "I do not believe

Supporters of Ravi rallied in front of the New Jersey Statehouse in May 2012.

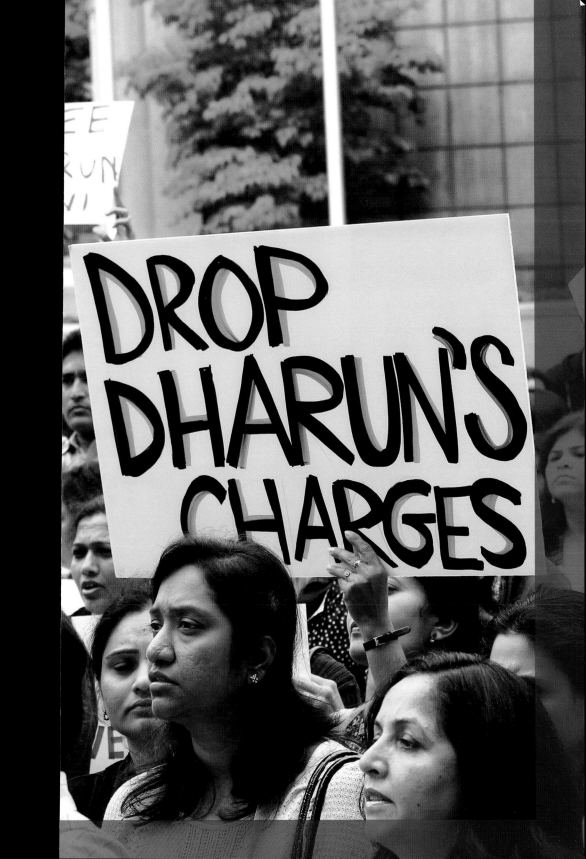

he hated Tyler Clementi. I do believe he acted out of colossal insensitivity."[7]

HATE SPEECH AND HATE CRIMES

Legal experts stress that hate crime laws punish actions, not thoughts, ideas, or protected expressions of ideas. But while hate speech itself is not illegal, police can still use hateful remarks or Internet postings uttered by a criminal to determine whether a crime is a hate crime. This fact has led to controversies about whether hate crime laws really do punish thoughts and beliefs rather than acts.

Political writer Jesse Larner, for example, believes existing hate crime laws can easily lead to laws that outlaw prejudiced thoughts and speech:

HATE CRIME LAWS AND RELIGIOUS EXPRESSION

One concern about the HCPA and other hate crime laws is that they threaten freedom of religious expression. The main objection centers on the addition of sexual orientation and gender identity to the protected classes of people. Many of those who oppose these additions believe the Bible condemns gay people. They worry religious leaders who speak out against gay people in sermons could be charged with hate crimes.

Such cases have emerged in Canada and elsewhere in the world, but they have not impacted religious expression in the United States. In 2012, the US Justice Department found "no credible threat of prosecution" for simply expressing a belief.[8]

Hate crime laws do set us up for hate speech laws. At present all of the model guides for hate crime laws require an 'underlying' crime. . . . But if speech or thought produces extra liability when paired with an underlying violent crime, it is but a small step to unpairing them, preserving the criminal liability of hate alone.[9]

Larner based part of his argument on the fact that hate speech has been outlawed in other democracies, such as Canada. However, attorney Michael Lieberman believes this cannot happen in the United States. "The United States is plainly not Canada—the First Amendment makes the United States unique," he wrote.[10]

CHAPTER NINE

COMBATING
HATE CRIMES

Hate crimes are combated through laws, law enforcement, education, public policy, and advocacy organizations. Legal and educational efforts to combat hate crimes focus on prevention, as well as on enforcing consequences of these crimes and helping victims heal.

COMMUNITY-BASED ACTIONS

Organizations such as the SPLC and ADL have been leaders in fighting hate crimes on many fronts, including advocacy, legal representation, education, and research. The SPLC and ADL sponsor education programs in which they send representatives to present

Attempts to pass hate crimes laws in the early 2000s, including a 2007 effort by Senator Gordon Smith, represented one way to fight hate crimes.

programs on tolerance and cooperation in schools and communities. They also train people of all ages to become leaders in advocating for tolerance and fighting against the bigotry that underlies hate crimes. Some programs focus on educating young people about recruitment tactics used by hate groups. These groups often recruit new members at high schools and colleges, as well as through social media. Awareness of these practices can help people beware of being lured.

Other programs involve law enforcement agencies working with community members to fight hate crimes. The Boston Police Department started the first such program in 1978. Its Community Disorders Unit educates police officers and the public about bias crimes and methods of stopping them. Its success with community-based policing led the Community Disorders Unit to serve as a model for community-based programs nationwide.

The national Community Relations Service (CRS) often helps state and local community-relations task forces get started. CRS sends representatives to localities experiencing problems with prejudice and bias crimes.

These representatives promote dialogue and understanding. According to Turpin-Petrosino, such programs are key to combating hate crimes. "Replacing fear and suspicion with the recognition that people are more similar than dissimilar will help build resistance to the *us vs. them* paradigm," she wrote.[1]

FIGHTING HATE GROUPS IN THE MILITARY

Other efforts to combat hate crimes aim to counteract hate group members who embed themselves in or recruit from the US military. In the late 1900s and early 2000s, some hate groups established branches near military bases to try to attract current and former service members. At the same time, these

RACIAL COOPERATION

Police in the 2000s are often accused of bias crimes against minorities. But the Boston Police Department is rarely involved in such bias issues. *Boston Globe* reporter Farah Stockman credits the 1978 founding of the Community Disorders Unit for this fact. It was established after more than 600 incidents of racial unrest and crime in Boston during the 1970s. Few thought the unit would be effective. "At that time . . . the police department . . . viewed racial harassment as a fact of life: unstoppable, inevitable, and random," Stockman wrote.[2]

But persistence from officers of all races led to productive, cooperative relationships with whites, blacks, gays, and other community groups. Stockman noted the unit facilitated "a sea change in police culture" that led to a similar change in community culture.[3] "I think we made people realize that [racial bias is] wrong," said officer Brian Flynn at a 2015 reunion of officers from the original team.[4]

groups encouraged existing members to join the military to receive weapons training that could benefit group assaults on selected targets. For example, in 1988, white supremacist T. J. Leyden of the group Hammerskin Nation joined the US Marine Corps. In his words, he joined "for one specific reason: I would learn how to shoot. I also learned how to use C-4 (explosives), [to] blow things up."[5] A 2008 report found half of the racist extremists in the US had military experience.[6]

One of the best-known neo-Nazi group members in the military was Wade Page. Page joined the US Army in 1992 and was sent to Fort Bragg, North Carolina, in 1995. At that time, he was not actively involved with hate groups. But according to an SPLC article, Fort Bragg "served as the home base for a brazen cadre of white supremacist soldiers. Nazi flags flew and party music endorsed the killing of African Americans and Jews."[7] Page became an avid member of the National Alliance group. The army discharged him for drunkenness in 1998, but he stayed involved with hate groups. He became angry at Muslims after the September 11, 2001, terrorist attacks. This led him to kill six Sikhs at a Sikh temple in Wisconsin on

Sikhs all over the country mourned the August 2012 murder of six people at a Sikh temple in Wisconsin.

August 5, 2012. Then he killed himself. Authorities believe he mistook the Sikhs for Muslims, perhaps because both Sikhs and Muslims often wear turbans and beards.

Military commanders launched investigations of hate group involvement in the armed services in 1996. In one investigation, a general in Fort Lewis, Washington, ordered 19,000 soldiers to undergo strip searches so officers could look for hate group tattoos.[8] Violators were dismissed. But soon, extended wars in Iraq and Afghanistan resulted in shortages in military personnel. Recruiters, loosening standards to fill these shortages, began knowingly recruiting and allowing hate group members and sympathizers to join the military, even though such individuals are officially banned.

In 2009 and 2012, the military reaffirmed its ban on hate group members. It also banned soldiers from blogging or chatting on racist websites while on duty. In response to assertions that military recruiters had become more tolerant of soldiers affiliated with hate groups, a spokeswoman for the Department of Defense noted, "Participation in extremist activities has never been tolerated and is punishable under the Uniform Code of Military Justice."[9] And in 2009, the Department of Homeland Security implemented Operation Vigilant Eagle. This program is meant to target and investigate military personnel returning from Iraq or Afghanistan who pose a risk for extremism and domestic terrorism. However, many veterans have complained about being placed under surveillance and even being arrested for posting opinions on Facebook that criticize the US government. This has led to investigations by civil liberties organizations.

"THE SOCIAL CONDITIONS OF THE PAST ARE DEEPLY ETCHED INTO THE SOCIAL AND CULTURAL NORMS OF TODAY."[10]

—CRIMINOLOGY PROFESSOR CAROLYN TURPIN-PETROSINO

THE PERSISTENCE OF HATE CRIMES

Despite ongoing efforts to punish and prevent hate crimes, these acts continue to occur regularly. The fact that approximately 260,000 hate crimes occur annually in the United States has led many people to question whether hate crime laws are effective.[11] The US government believes they have helped. On May 15, 2013, Attorney General Eric Holder told Congress the HCPA has "improved our ability to safeguard our civil rights and pursue justice for those who are victimized because of their gender, sexual orientation, gender identity, or disability."[12] Holder emphasized that between the HCPA's passage in 2009 and 2013, the Justice

ARE HATE CRIME LAWS EFFECTIVE?

The 45 US states with hate crime laws believe the penalty enhancements in these laws deter at least some people from acting on prejudices and committing hate crimes. ADL attorney Michael Lieberman agrees with this contention. "If you're going to burn a swastika into the side of a synagogue or burn a cross and demonstrate your hatred that way, if you know that you're going to be doing serious time for that, then you may modify your behavior," he states.[14]

However, it is difficult to assess whether hate crime laws are actually effective. The number of hate crimes has not declined since these laws were enacted. Lieberman suggests this may be because people are more likely to report hate crimes when they know laws exist to do something about a crime.

Department convicted 44 people in 16 states under this law.[13]

But many people believe other measures are needed to help fight hate crimes. Even with hate crime laws and progress in racial relations, the same groups that have been historically subjected to bias acts see ongoing evidence of institutional and personal hatred in the 2000s. In 2010, for example, several Tea Party supporters protesting health-care reforms in Washington, DC, spat on black congressmen and yelled racial taunts. They also heckled Congressman Barney Frank, who is gay. In 2015, the Charleston murders shared headlines with many other bias acts. Perhaps this is why President Obama made the following remark in a speech after the Charleston massacre. "It is not good enough to simply show sympathy. We as a people have got to change," he said.[15]

"I HAVE HEARD THINGS TODAY THAT I HAVE NOT HEARD SINCE MARCH 15, 1960, WHEN I WAS MARCHING TO GET OFF THE BACK OF THE BUS."[16]

—CONGRESSMAN JAMES CLYBURN ON MARCH 20, 2010, AFTER BEING ASSAULTED WITH RACIAL SLURS DURING A PROTEST AGAINST HEALTH-CARE REFORMS

Mourners were emotional during President Obama's speech at a memorial service in Charleston.

FROM THE HEADLINES

THE ORLANDO NIGHTCLUB SHOOTING

On June 12, 2016, Omar Mateen entered a crowded nightclub in Orlando, Florida. The club, called Pulse, was popular in the local gay community. It was the club's Latin Night, and most of the patrons were Hispanic. Mateen, armed with a semiautomatic rifle and a pistol, opened fire. He killed 49 people and wounded dozens more.[17] After a lengthy standoff with police, Mateen was shot and killed. It was the deadliest mass shooting in US history.

Mateen asserted that he was acting against the United States on behalf of the terrorist group ISIS, but the act was also seen as a hate crime against gay people. The gunman's father, Seddique Mir Mateen, said his son had been outraged after seeing gay men kissing in public. Mateen had grown up in the United States, and people who knew him as a teenager said he had been comfortable around gay people. But more recent testimony from his ex-wife and coworkers suggested he was known to have exhibited violence, racism, and homophobia.

President Obama referred to the attack as both a terrorist act and a hate crime. Georgia State professor Mia Bloom agreed, noting that "it doesn't have to be one thing at the exclusion of others. It was definitely a hate crime, and it was an act of terrorism."[18]

Mourners set up memorials and gathered together outside Pulse.

ESSENTIAL
FACTS

MAJOR EVENTS

- On October 28, 2009, the Matthew Shepard and James Byrd Jr. Hate Crimes Prevention Act (HCPA) is signed into law.

- On June 17, 2015, Dylann Roof shoots and kills nine people and injures one during a Bible study session at the Emanuel AME Church in Charleston, South Carolina.

- On June 12, 2016, Omar Mateen shoots and kills 49 people in an attack on a gay nightclub in Orlando, Florida.

KEY PLAYERS

- The Federal Bureau of Investigation and the Bureau of Justice Statistics track US hate crimes.

- The Southern Poverty Law Center tracks hate groups in the United States.

- The Anti-Defamation League created a model hate crime statute to serve as a basis for anti-hate crime laws.

IMPACT ON SOCIETY

The history of hate crimes in America dates back to the nation's earliest days, when prejudice against blacks, Native Americans, and other minorities led to widespread discrimination, the practice of slavery, and murder. Often these incidents were either directly supported or ignored by the government. In the mid-1900s, the civil rights movement brought about laws targeting this type of discrimination. Since then, the US government has stepped up efforts to combat crimes based on bias or hate. These efforts led to the Hate Crimes Prevention Act, passed in 2009. However, politicians continue to argue about how to determine whether a crime is based on hate, whether such crimes should carry harsher penalties, and where the line between free speech and illegal hate speech lies.

QUOTE

"Free expression protects the right to express offensive views but not the right to behave criminally."

—Attorney and hate crimes expert Frederick Lawrence

GLOSSARY

BUREAUCRACY

The body of officials and administrators of a government.

CRIMINOLOGIST

An expert in law and criminal behavior.

DEFAMATION

The act of damaging someone's reputation through false statements.

DEPORTATION

The expulsion of a person from a country through a legal process.

EPITHET

An abusive term; a slur.

FELONY

A crime more serious than a misdemeanor, usually punishable by imprisonment.

HOMOPHOBIA
Fear and hostility toward homosexuals.

MISDEMEANOR
A crime with less serious penalties than those assessed for a felony.

NEO-NAZI
A person with extreme racist and nationalistic views, whose ideology stems from the Nazi regime that controlled Germany in the 1930s and early 1940s.

PREJUDICE
An unfair feeling of dislike for a person or group because of race, sex, or religion.

SOCIOLOGIST
A person who studies the development, structure, and functioning of human society.

STATUTE
A law.

SUPREMACIST
Someone who believes people of a particular race, religion, or other category are better than other people.

VIGILANTE
A person who attempts to enforce the law in a community but has no legal authority to do so.

ADDITIONAL
RESOURCES

SELECTED BIBLIOGRAPHY

Bell, Jeannine. *Policing Hatred*. New York: New York UP, 2002. Print.

Levin, Jack, and Jack McDevitt. *Hate Crimes Revisited: America's War on Those Who Are Different*. Boulder, CO: Westview, 2002. Print.

Turpin-Petrosino, Carolyn. *Understanding Hate Crimes*. New York: Routledge, 2015. Print.

FURTHER READINGS

Bartoletti, Susan Campbell. *They Called Themselves the K.K.K.: The Birth of an American Terrorist Group*. New York: Houghton, 2014. Print.

Bruce, Judith. *Hate Crimes*. Farmington Hills, MI: Greenhaven, 2009. Print.

Streissguth, Thomas. *Hate Crimes*. New York: Facts On File, 2009. Print.

WEBSITES

To learn more about Special Reports, visit **booklinks.abdopublishing.com**. These links are routinely monitored and updated to provide the most current information available.

FOR MORE INFORMATION

For more information on this subject, contact or visit the following organizations:

California State University, San Bernardino Center for the Study of Hate and Extremism
5500 University Parkway
San Bernardino, CA 92407
909-537-7771
http://hatemonitor.csusb.edu
The Center for the Study of Hate and Extremism is a research and policy center that studies how prejudice and terrorism impact society and how education, laws, and policy can help mitigate these challenges.

Southern Poverty Law Center
400 Washington Avenue
Montgomery, AL 36104
888-414-7752
http://www.splcenter.org
The Southern Poverty Law Center is a nonprofit organization dedicated to fighting hatred and bigotry and seeking justice for vulnerable members of society. It is active in education, advocacy, and legal representation, and it tracks hate crimes and hate groups.

SOURCE NOTES

CHAPTER 1. THE CHARLESTON MASSACRE

1. Robert Costa, et al. "Dylann Roof Captured amid Hate Crime Investigation." *Washington Post.* Washington Post, 18 June 2015. Web. 1 Sept. 2016.

2. Matt Apuzzo. "Dylan Roof Is Indicted on Federal Hate Crime Charges." *New York Times.* New York Times, 22 July 2015. Web. 1 Sept. 2016.

3. Frances Robles and Nikita Stewart. "Dylann Roof's Past." *New York Times.* New York Times, 16 July 2015. Web. 1 Sept. 2016.

4. Andrew Knapp. "Aftermath of Charleston Church Slayings." *Post and Courier.* Post and Courier, 19 June 2015. Web. 1 Sept. 2016.

5. Ibid.

6. Ibid.

7. Ibid.

8. Scott Neuman. "Photos of Dylann Roof." *NPR.* NPR, 20 June 2015. Web. 1 Sept. 2016.

9. Andrew Knapp. "Aftermath of Charleston Church Slayings." *Post and Courier.* Post and Courier, 19 June 2015. Web. 1 Sept. 2016.

10. Catherine E. Shoichet and Evan Perez. "Dylann Roof Faces Hate Crime Charges in Charleston Shooting." *CNN.* CNN, 22 July 2015. Web. 1 Sept. 2016.

11. "Confederate Flag Removed from South Carolina Capitol Grounds." *Huffington Post.* Huffington Post, 10 July 2015. Web. 1 Sept. 2016.

12. David Greenwald. "Charleston Church Shooting Triggers a Variety of Different Reactions." *Davis Vanguard.* Davis Vanguard, 20 June 2015. Web. 1 Sept. 2016.

13. 'We Affirm That All Black Lives Matter." *Black Lives Matter.* Black Lives Matter, n.d. Web. 12 May 2016.

CHAPTER 2. WHAT ARE HATE CRIMES?

1. "Latest Hate Crime Statistics." *FBI.* FBI, 16 Nov. 2015. Web. 18 May 2016.

2. "Hate Incidents." *Southern Poverty Law Center.* SPLC, n.d. Web. 18 May 2016.

3. Christina A. Cassidy. "AP: Patchy Reporting Undercuts National Hate Crimes Count." *ABC News.* ABC News, 6 June 2016. Web. 1 Sept. 2016.

4. Ibid.

5. Eric Heisig. "Busted Glass Door Yields Hate Crime Charge." *Houma Today.* Houma Today, 19 Apr. 2011. Web. 24 May 2016.

6. Lauren Steinbrecher. "Vandalism of Pride Flag in Midvale May Constitute Hate Crime." *Fox13 Salt Lake City.* Fox13 Salt Lake City, 16 Apr. 2016. Web. 1 Sept. 2016.

7. Jorge Valencia. "What Is a Hate Crime?" *WUNC.* WUNC, 19 Feb. 2015. Web. 1 Sept. 2016.

8. "Hate Groups." *Southern Poverty Law Center.* SPLC, n.d. Web. 18 May 2016.

9. Jack Levin and Jack McDevitt. "Hate Crimes Revisited." Boulder, CO: Westview, 2002. Print. 106.

10. "Jewish Man Attacked at Brooklyn College." *ABC*. ABC, 24 Dec. 2015. Web. 1 Sept. 2016.

11. "Latest Hate Crime Statistics." *FBI*. FBI, 16 Nov. 2015. Web. 18 May 2016.

12. Frederick Lawrence. *Punishing Hate*. Cambridge, MA: Harvard, 1999. Print. 40.

13. Ibid.

14. "New Details Emerge in Matthew Shepard's Murder." *ABC News*. ABC News, 26 Nov. 2004. Web. 1 Sept. 2016.

CHAPTER 3. WHY DO HATE CRIMES OCCUR?

1. Joe R. Feagin. *Racist America*. New York: Routledge, 2001. Print. 100.

2. Ibid. 101.

3. Michael E. Miller. "Attacks on Muslims across the Country." *Washington Post*. Washington Post, 10 Dec. 2015. Web. 1 Sept. 2016.

4. Terri Yuh-lin Chen. "Hate Violence as Border Patrol." *Asian American Law Journal*. Asian American Law Journal, Jan. 2000. Web. 1 Sept. 2016.

5. Michael E. Miller. "Attacks on Muslims across the Country." *Washington Post*. Washington Post, 10 Dec. 2015. Web. 1 Sept. 2016.

6. Harold Brackman. "Anti-Semitism: A Clear and Present Danger." *Simon Wiesenthal Center*. Simon Wiesenthal Center, 12 June 2015. Web. 1 Sept. 2016.

7. Jennifer Sullivan. "Seattle Jewish Center Shooter Gets Life Sentence." *Los Angeles Times*. Los Angeles Times, 15 Jan. 2010. Web. 1 Sept. 2016.

8. Howard J. Ehrlich. *Hate Crimes and Ethnoviolence*. Boulder, CO: Westview, 2009. Print. 5.

9. Thomas G. Dyer. *Theodore Roosevelt and the Idea of Race*. Baton Rouge, LA: Louisiana State UP, 1980. Print. 109–110.

10. "T. J. Leyden." *Forgiveness Project*. FP, 3 Aug. 2011. Web. 1 Sept. 2016.

11. Howard J. Ehrlich. *Hate Crimes and Ethnoviolence*. Boulder, CO: Westview, 2009. Print. 28.

12. "Elderly Neo-Nazi Gives Nazi Salute as He Faces Death Penalty." *New York Daily News*. New York Daily News, 1 Sept. 2015. Web. 1 Sept. 2016.

13. Sonia Scherr. "Children of Extremists." *SPLC*. SPLC, 30 Nov. 2009. Web. 1 Sept. 2016.

14. Carolyn Turpin-Petrosino. *Understanding Hate Crimes*. New York: Routledge, 2015. Print. 149.

15. "T. J. Leyden Tells His Story." *SPLC*. SPLC, 15 Mar. 1998. Web. 1 May 2016.

CHAPTER 4. THE HISTORY OF HATE CRIMES IN AMERICA

1. Benjamin Madley. "California's Yuki Indians: Defining Genocide in Native American History." *Western Historical Quarterly* 9 (Autumn 2008): 309. Print. 309.

2. Gayle Olson-Raymer. "Whose Manifest Destiny?" *Humboldt State University*. Humboldt State University, n.d. Web. 24 May 2016.

3. Ibid.

4. "Park Ethnography Program." *NPS*. NPS, n.d. Web. 2 Sept. 2016.

5. Gayle Olson-Raymer. "Whose Manifest Destiny?" *Humboldt State University*. Humboldt State University, n.d. Web. 24 May 2016.

6. Ralph Ginzburg. *100 Years of Lynchings*. Baltimore, MD: Black Classic, 1962. Print. 151–153.

7. Ibid. 153.

8. Peter Jacobs. "The Lynching of a Jewish Man in Georgia 100 Years Ago Changed America Forever." *Business Insider*. BI, 18 Aug. 2015. Web. 27 Apr. 2016.

9. Ibid.

10. David M. P. Freund. *Colored Property*. Chicago: U of Chicago P, 2007 Print. 14.

11. Michael Hannon. "People v. Ossian Sweet." *UMN Law Library*. UMN, n.d. Web. 29 Apr. 2016.

12. Ibid.

13. David Chalmers. "The KKK." *SPLC*. SPLC, 25 Jan. 2010. Web. 25 May 2016.

CHAPTER 5. THE EVOLUTION OF HATE CRIME LAWS

1. "State v. Miller." *Leagle*. Leagle, n.d. Web. 3 May 2016.

2. Carolyn Turpin-Petrosino. *Understanding Hate Crimes*. New York: Routledge, 2015. Print. 67.

3. "Senate Apologizes for Inaction." *NBC*. NBC, 13 June 2005. Web. 26 May 2016.

4. Tim Konhaus. "'I Thought Things Would Be Different There.'" *West Virginia History: A Journal of Regional Studies*, vol. 1, no. 2, Fall 2007, 27.

5. "Southern Manifesto." *History*. US House of Representatives, n.d. Web. 2 Sept. 2016.

SOURCE NOTES
CONTINUED

6. Carolyn Turpin-Petrosino. *Understanding Hate Crimes.* New York: Routledge, 2015. Print. 17.

7. *Congressional Record: Proceedings and Debates of the 111th Congress First Session,* vol. 155, part 8. Washington, DC: US GPO, 2009. Print. 11082.

8. Ibid. 11087.

CHAPTER 6. THE NATURE OF MODERN HATE CRIME LAWS

1. "14th Amendment." *Legal Information Institute.* Cornell University, n.d. Web. 18 May 2016.

2. Ave Mince Didier. "Is Everyone Protected by Hate Crime Laws?" *Criminal Defense Lawyer.* Criminal Defense Lawyer, n.d. Web. 2 May 2016.

3. Carolyn Turpin-Petrosino. *Understanding Hate Crimes.* New York: Routledge, 2015. Print. 57.

4. "939.645 Penalty." *Wisconsin State Legislature.* Wisconsin, n.d. Web. 18 May 2016.

5. "RAV v. City of St. Paul." *Oyez.* Kent College of Law, n.d. Web. 2 Sept. 2016.

6. Geoffrey R. Stone and Eugene Volokh. "Freedom of Speech and the Press." *National Constitution Center.* NCR, n.d. Web. 26 Apr. 2016.

7. Michael Lieberman. "Hate Crime Laws: Punishment to Fit the Crime." *Dissent.* Dissent, Summer 2010. Web. 3 June 2016.

8. *Congressional Record: Proceedings and Debates of the 111th Congress First Session,* vol. 155, part 8. Washington, DC: US GPO, 2009. Print. 11082.

9. Wade Henderson. "Bias Laws Ensure Action against Hate." *New York Times.* New York Times, 7 Mar. 2012. Web. 3 May 2016.

10. Greg Hilburn. "'Blue Lives Matter' Bill Expected to Become Law in LA." *USA Today.* USA Today, 24 May 2016. Web. 2 Sept. 2016.

11. "ADL Opposes 'Blue Lives Matter' Bill." *ADL.* ADL, n.d. Web. 2 May 2016.

12. Ibid.

13. Greg Hilburn. "'Blue Lives Matter' Bill Expected to Become Law in LA." *USA Today.* USA Today, 24 May 2016. Web. 2 Sept. 2016.

14. "ADL Opposes 'Blue Lives Matter' Bill." *ADL.* ADL, n.d. Web. 2 May 2016.

CHAPTER 7. ARE HATE CRIME LAWS NECESSARY?

1. "18 Years for Brooklyn Heights Bomber." *New York Post.* New York Post, 26 Feb. 2010. Web. 22 Apr. 2016.

2. James Doubek. "How Well Do Hate Crime Laws Really Work?" *National Public Radio.* NPR, n.d. Web. 28 June 2015.

3. Jorge Valencia. "What Is a Hate Crime?" *WUNC.* WUNC, 19 Feb. 2015. Web. 18 May 2016.

4. James B. Jacobs and Kimberly Potter. *Hate Crimes.* New York: Oxford UP, 1998. Print. 8.

5. Ibid. 131.

6. Ibid. 5.

7. Ibid. 131.

8. Ibid.

9. *Congressional Record: Proceedings and Debates of the 111th Congress First Session*, vol. 155, part 8. Washington, DC: US GPO, 2009. Print. 11082.

10. Ibid. 11087.

11. Tish Durkin. "Focus on the Crime, Not the Victim." *New York Times*. New York Times, 7 Mar. 2012. Web. 3 May 2016.

12. "Latest Hate Crime Statistics Available." *FBI*. FBI, 16 Nov. 2015. Web. 18 May 2016.

13. Carolyn Turpin-Petrosino. *Understanding Hate Crimes*. New York: Routledge, 2015. Print. 3.

14. "Two Kentucky Men Acquitted." *CBS News*. CBS News, 24 Oct. 2012. Web. 2 Sept. 2016.

CHAPTER 8. FREE SPEECH AND HATE SPEECH

1. Frederick Lawrence. *Punishing Hate*. Cambridge, MA: Harvard, 1999. Print. 83.

2. Carolyn Turpin-Petrosino. *Understanding Hate Crimes*. New York: Routledge, 2015. Print. 12.

3. Frederick Lawrence. *Punishing Hate*. Cambridge, MA: Harvard, 1999. Print. 83.

4. Carolyn Turpin-Petrosino. *Understanding Hate Crimes*. New York: Routledge, 2015. Print. 23.

5. Michael Lieberman. "Hate Crime Laws." *Dissent*. Dissent, Summer 2010. Web. 3 June 2016.

6. Ian Parker. "The Story of a Suicide." *New Yorker*. New Yorker, 6 Feb. 2012. Web. 18 May 2016.

7. Kate Zernike. "Webcam-Spying Defendant Sentenced." *New York Times*. New York Times, 21 May 2012. Web. 2 Sept. 2016.

8. "Glenn, et al. v. Holder." *US Department of Justice*. US DoJ, 2 Aug. 2012. Web. 3 June 2016.

9. Jesse Larner. "Hate Crime/Thought Crime." *Dissent*. Dissent, Spring 2010. Web. 3 June 2010.

10. Michael Lieberman. "Hate Crime Laws." *Dissent*. Dissent, Summer 2010. Web. 3 June 2016.

CHAPTER 9. COMBATING HATE CRIMES

1. Carolyn Turpin-Petrosino. *Understanding Hate Crimes*. New York: Routledge, 2015. Print. 229.

2. Farah Stockman. "What a Small Boston Police Unit Can Teach about Changing Culture." *Boston Globe*. Boston Globe, 7 Sept. 2015. Web. 2 Sept. 2016.

3. Ibid.

4. Ibid.

5. Daniel Trotto. "US Army Fights Racists within Its Own Ranks." *Reuters*. Reuters, 21 Aug. 2012. Web. 2 Sept. 2016.

6. Ibid.

7. Marilyn Elias. "Sikh Temple Killer Radicalized in Army." *SPLC*. SPLC, 11 Nov. 2012. Web. 24 May 2016.

8. Carolyn Turpin-Petrosino. *Understanding Hate Crimes*. New York: Routledge, 2015. Print. 39–40.

9. Daniel Trotto. "US Army Fights Racists within Its Own Ranks." *Reuters*. Reuters, 21 Aug. 2012. Web. 2 Sept. 2016.

10. Carolyn Turpin-Petrosino. *Understanding Hate Crimes*. New York: Routledge, 2015. Print. 44.

11. "Hate Incidents." *SPLC*. SPLC, n.d. Web. 18 May 2016.

12. Jocelyn Samuels. "Commemorating the Fourth Anniversary of the Shepard-Byrd Hate Crime Prevention Act." *White House*. White House, 28 Oct. 2013. Web. 2 Sept. 2016.

13. Ibid.

14. James Doubek. "How Well Do Hate Crime Laws Really Work?" *NPR*. NPR, n.d. Web. 28 June 2015.

15. Andrew Knapp. "Aftermath of Charleston Church Slayings." *Post and Courier*. Post and Courier, 19 June 2015. Web. 1 Sept. 2016.

16. Paul Kane. "Protesters Accused of Spitting on Lawmaker." *Washington Post*. Washington Post, 20 Mar. 2010. Web. 1 May 2016.

17. "Florida Shooting." *New York Times*. New York Times, 14 June 2016. Web. 2 Sept. 2016.

18. Christopher Woolf and Matthew Bell. "What Do We Call the Attack in Orlando?" *PRI*. PRI, 13 June 2016. Web. 2 Sept. 2016.

INDEX

ABOUT THE
AUTHOR

Melissa Abramovitz is an award-winning freelance writer who specializes in educational nonfiction magazine articles and books for children and teenagers. She graduated from the University of California, San Diego, with a degree in psychology and is also a graduate of the Institute of Children's Literature.